AMERICA
The Beautiful

To my dear friends and classmates from Aurora West High, class of 1962.
You are the soul of the Heartland and the Spirit of America —W. M.

WENDELL MINOR

AMERICA

The Beautiful

POEM BY KATHARINE LEE BATES

PUFFIN BOOKS

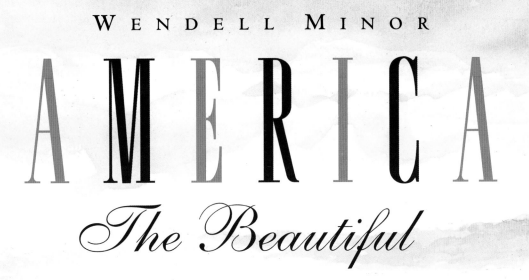

WENDELL MINOR

AMERICA
The Beautiful

POEM BY KATHARINE LEE BATES

PUFFIN BOOKS

INTRODUCTION
America The Beautiful

In 1893 Katharine Lee Bates journeyed from her Cape Cod home by train, west to Colorado. It was a trip that would change her life and change America.

It was the first time the young poet and professor of English experienced the diversity and vastness of our great land. She kept a diary in which she expressed her thoughts about what she saw. One day she trekked to the summit of Pikes Peak and would later record in that diary impressions of the excitement she felt about the magnificent view. Those diary jottings were the beginning of an idea for the poem "America the Beautiful."

For more than a century Americans have been singing the inspiring words to Katharine Lee Bates's poem with great love for our country. "America the Beautiful" means something special to each and every one of us. We conjure up images as we sing, and I'm certain that each of us has a unique vision.

The paintings in this book are the images that come to my mind when I sing the words. I think about all the beautiful places I have visited in my travels across the United States. I think about the poem's timeless message, and how it reminds me of America's history and those who have contributed to America's greatness.

It is my sincerest wish that Katharine Lee Bates's words and my paintings will serve as a reminder, to children and parents, of America's gifts. May you always enjoy her natural beauty and help preserve it. May you feel her pride of spirit, and may you make your own contributions to keep America great!

WENDELL MINOR

O beautiful for spacious skies,

For amber waves of grain,

For purple
mountain majesties
Above the fruited plain!

America!

America!

God shed His grace on thee

And crown thy good with brotherhood

From sea to shining sea!

O beautiful for pilgrim feet,

Whose stern, impassioned stress

A thoroughfare
for freedom beat
Across the wilderness!

America!

America!

God mend thine every flaw,
Confirm thy soul in self-control,
Thy liberty in law!

O beautiful for heroes proved
In liberating strife,
Who more than self their country loved,
And mercy more than life!

America!

America!

May God thy gold refine Till all success

be nobleness And every gain divine!

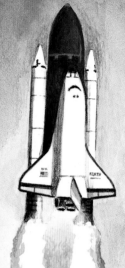

O beautiful for patriot dream

That sees beyond the years

Thine alabaster
cities gleam
Undimmed
by human tears!

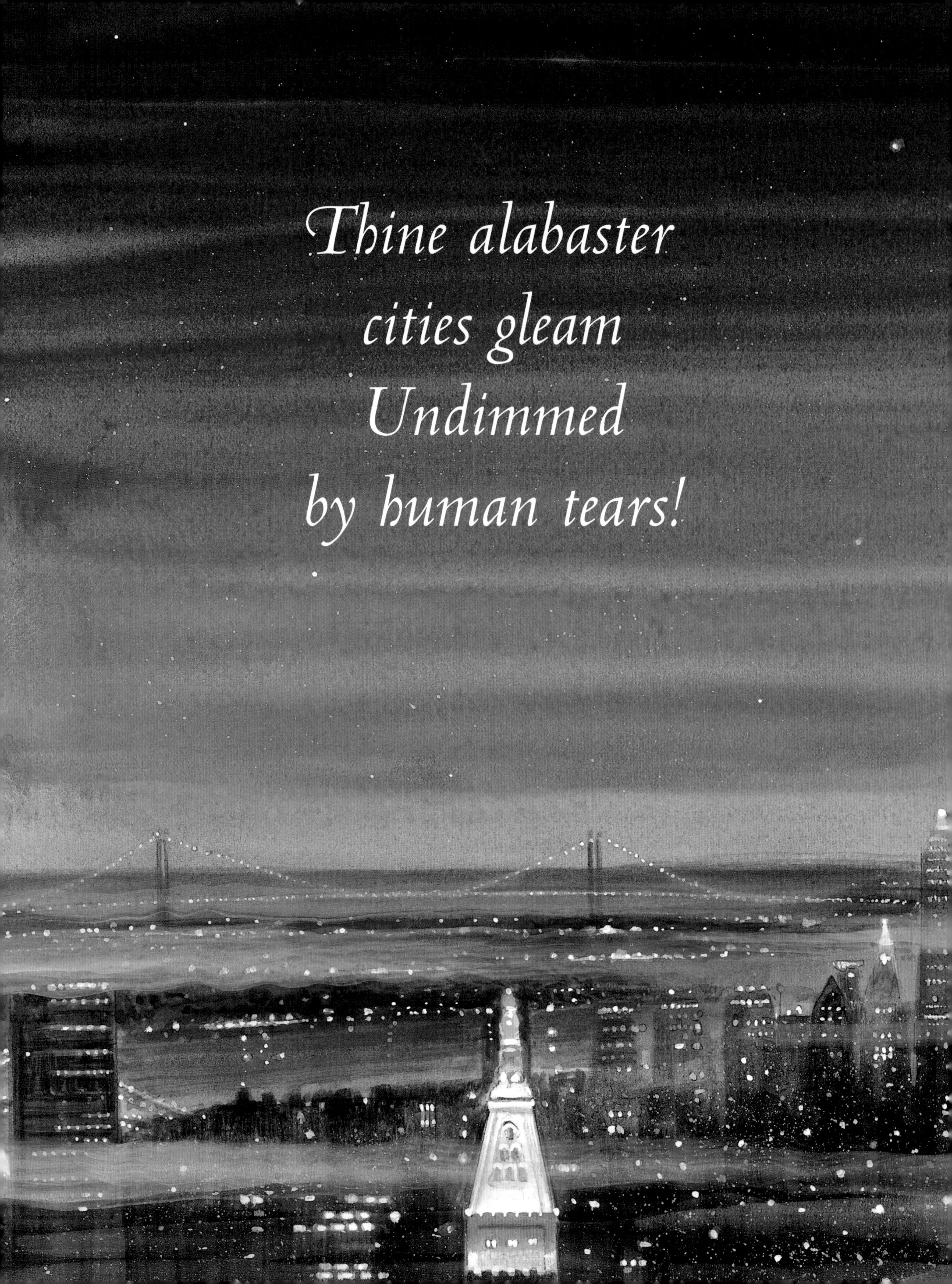

America!

America!

God shed His grace on thee

And crown thy good with brotherhood

From sea to shining sea!

Katharine Lee Bates

Katharine Lee Bates was born in 1859 in Falmouth, Massachusetts, where she started keeping a journal at the age of six. When she was twelve, she moved to Wellesley, Massachusetts, and, at eighteen, enrolled in the new, highly esteemed Wellesley College. She excelled in academics, wrote poetry for supplemental income and, after graduation, taught high school. In 1885, she returned to Wellesley as an English professor and became head of the English literature department in 1891.

Bates was known for her intelligence, wit and sense of humor, and was involved in numerous political and social reform organizations, among them the League of Nations and the Antivivisection Society. She helped form the New England Poetry Club in 1915, and was its first president. Her books include literary criticism, poetry, children's books and travelogues, the latter based on several trips to Europe and the Middle East.

In 1893, at thirty-three years of age, Bates embarked on a life-changing trip to Colorado to teach summer school, stopping at Niagara Falls and the futuristic "White City" of the World's Columbian Exposition in Chicago. At the end of the school term, she visited the summit of Pikes Peak. It was the breathtaking view from this place that inspired the words to "America the Beautiful." She submitted the poem for publication in 1895, when it appeared in *The Congregationalist*.

The poem's admirers determined it should be a hymn, so Bates revised it in 1904 and 1911 to make it easier to sing. People across the country sent melodies, but she stayed out of that debate, only requiring that the words not be altered. She continued to write and teach, making time to correspond with her fans, whose letters took up their own cabinet in her house. She died in 1929.

Since 1926, there has been talk of making "America the Beautiful," set to Ward's "Materna," the United States' national anthem. And to this day, the song remains one of the most beloved in the country.

And crown thy good with brotherhood

Samuel Augustus Ward

Samuel Augustus Ward's first instrument was the accordion, which he started playing when he was six years old. Born in 1848 in Newark, New Jersey, he never had formal music training, yet as a teenager he already had his own piano students. At age sixteen, he was the organist of a Manhattan church. Ward opened a successful music store, and in 1871, married Virginia Ward. They had four daughters. He became the organist at Grace Episcopal Church in Newark, and in 1889, founded Newark's Orpheus Club, a men's chorus that is still active. Ward composed music for the group and conducted it for fourteen years. He is remembered for his energy and passion.

Like Bates, Ward was thirty-three years old when a trip to a beautiful American site inspired him. On the steamboat ride home after a visit to Coney Island, he started humming a tune. But he had no paper, so the melody he would be remembered for first appeared on his friend's shirt cuff. Ward called the tune "Materna," and used it as a new setting for the hymn "O Mother Dear Jerusalem." A five-cent church weekly published it in 1888. It was later adopted in several hymnals. In 1904, his melody and Bates's lyrics were put together for singing, and in 1910 they were published as the song we know today.

Ward died in 1903, never knowing that his melody for "America the Beautiful" would become the nation's favorite. However, new versions kept appearing. In 1926, the National Federation of Music Clubs held a contest to choose an official tune written specifically for the poem. Over nine hundred entries were submitted, but there was no winner. Ward's composition continues to stand the test of time.

Sources:
—*America the Beautiful: The Stirring True Story Behind Our Nation's Favorite Song*, by Lynn Sherr (PublicAffairs, 2001)
—Wellesley College
—The Falmouth Historical Society

America The Beautiful

KATHARINE LEE BATES

SAMUEL A. WARD

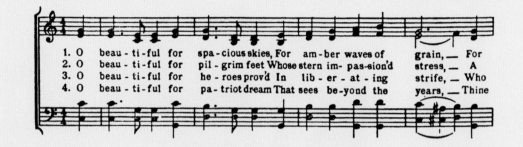

1. O beau-ti-ful for spa-cious skies, For am-ber waves of grain, — For
2. O beau-ti-ful for pil-grim feet Whose stern im-pas-sion'd stress, — A
3. O beau-ti-ful for he-roes prov'd In lib-er-at-ing strife, — Who
4. O beau-ti-ful for pa-triot dream That sees be-yond the years, — Thine

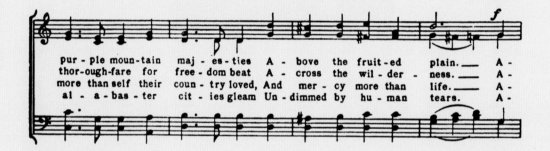

pur-ple moun-tain maj-es-ties A-bove the fruit-ed plain. — A-
thor-ough-fare for free-dom beat A-cross the wil-der-ness. — A-
more than self their coun-try loved, And mer-cy more than life. — A-
al-a-bas-ter cit-ies gleam Un-dimmed by hu-man tears. — A-

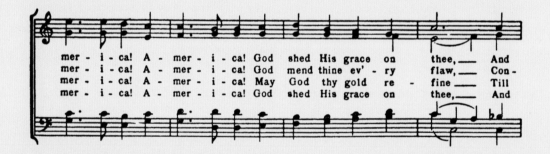

mer-i-ca! A-mer-i-ca! God shed His grace on thee, — And
mer-i-ca! A-mer-i-ca! God mend thine ev'-ry flaw, — Con-
mer-i-ca! A-mer-i-ca! May God thy gold re-fine — Till
mer-i-ca! A-mer-i-ca! God shed His grace on thee, — And

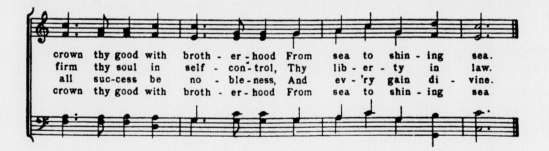

crown thy good with broth-er-hood From sea to shin-ing sea.
firm thy soul in self-con-trol, Thy lib-er-ty in law.
all suc-cess be no-ble-ness, And ev-'ry gain di-vine.
crown thy good with broth-er-hood From sea to shin-ing sea

The poem paired with Ward's melody as it first appeared in many church hymnals.

America the Beautiful

O beautiful for spacious skies,
For amber waves of grain,
For purple mountain majesties
Above the fruited plain!
America! America!
God shed His grace on thee
And crown thy good with brotherhood
From sea to shining sea!

O beautiful for pilgrim feet
Whose stern, impassioned stress
A thoroughfare for freedom beat
Across the wilderness!
America! America!
God mend thine every flaw,
Confirm thy soul in self-control,
Thy liberty in law!

An example of one of the many handwritten copies of the poem Katharine Lee Bates penned in her lifetime.

AMERICA
The Beautiful
A SENSE OF TIME AND PLACE

Cover

WASHINGTON, CONNECTICUT ♦ The hand-painted American flag on this rural mailbox is in the town where I live. It reminds me of many rural towns in America where home is a beautiful place to be.

Half Title Page

YOSEMITE NATIONAL PARK, CALIFORNIA ♦ Half Dome is one of many famous landmarks in Yosemite National Park. In 1864 President Abraham Lincoln was the first president ever to set aside land for preservation. He signed a bill which designated Yosemite Valley as a place to be preserved for all time.

Title Page

NIAGARA FALLS, NEW YORK ♦ Katharine Lee Bates visited Niagara Falls in the summer of 1893. This view of the falls has been a very popular tourist attraction for more than 150 years.

Introduction

PIKES PEAK, COLORADO ♦ The Garden of the Gods forms the gateway to Pikes Peak, the Rocky Mountain summit that inspired Katharine Lee Bates to write "America the Beautiful." Today nearly six million visitors a year thrill to the same view that inspired her great poem.

O beautiful for spacious skies,

KANSAS ♦ On her train trip across America, Katharine Lee Bates was impressed by the golden wheat fields of Kansas. On the Great Plains, the sky often seems to be as dominant as the land itself.

For purple mountain majesties

GRAND TETON NATIONAL PARK, WYOMING ♦ When I first saw the Grand Tetons in Wyoming, I felt inspired to sing Katharine Lee Bates's words, "For purple mountain majesties . . ."

America! America! / God shed His grace on thee

VERMONT ♦ Weather vanes, made by craftsmen in the eighteenth and early nineteenth centuries, can still be seen in many New England towns. This one seems to herald the brilliant colors of autumn.

And crown thy good with brotherhood

HECETA HEAD, OREGON ♦ Heceta Head Lighthouse provides a spectacular view of the Oregon coast and the Pacific Ocean. Heceta Head is named in honor of Don Bruno de Heceta of the Spanish Royal Navy, who explored and charted the region about 1775.

O beautiful for pilgrim feet,

PLYMOUTH, MASSACHUSETTS ♦ Plimoth Plantation is a reconstruction of the original Pilgrim settlement of 1627. Visitors can get a sense of what life was like for one of the first colonies in a new land.

A thoroughfare for freedom beat

SCOTTS BLUFF NATIONAL MONUMENT, NEBRASKA ♦ After the Gold Rush of 1849, tens of thousands of pioneers trekked west in covered wagons through Mitchell Pass along the famous Oregon Trail, on their way to California. This site has come to symbolize America's pioneer spirit.

America! America!

NORTH OF NATCHEZ, MISSISSIPPI ♦ The Mississippi River borders ten states in the heartland of America. It begins in Minnesota and carries 350 million gallons of freshwater to the Gulf of Mexico every day. The Mississippi River became part of the United States when President Thomas Jefferson arranged the Louisiana Purchase in 1803.

God mend thine every flaw,

IOWA ♦ During the Great Depression of the 1930s, farmers in Iowa harvested more than 440,000 acres of wheat; today less than 20,000 acres of winter wheat are cultivated. Corn and soybeans are now the leading crops in the state.

O beautiful for heroes proved

MOUNT RUSHMORE NATIONAL MEMORIAL, SOUTH DAKOTA Created by sculptor Gutzon Borglum, Mount Rushmore depicts four presidents: George Washington, Thomas Jefferson, Theodore Roosevelt, and Abraham Lincoln. Work on the memorial began in 1927 and was completed in 1941.

America! America!

THE HILL COUNTRY, TEXAS ♦ Texas's state flower, the blue-bonnet, blooms in the spring and brings a glorious bluish purple hue to the landscape of central Texas. The ever-present windmills that pump water to livestock are a constant reminder of Texas's ranching heritage.

May God thy gold refine

KITTY HAWK, NORTH CAROLINA ♦ The Wright brothers from Dayton, Ohio, created and built the first mechanically powered aircraft. Their plane first flew in December 1903, and was a noble success! Today, the 1903 Wright Flyer can be seen at the National Air and Space Museum in Washington, D.C.

O beautiful for patriot dream

KENNEDY SPACE CENTER, CAPE CANAVERAL, FLORIDA Only sixty-six years after the first powered flight, men landed on the moon! NASA's shuttle now lifts off from the Kennedy Space Center, located within a wildlife refuge, Canaveral National Seashore. Our national symbol, the American bald eagle, makes its home there, too.

Thine alabaster cities gleam

NEW YORK CITY ♦ "Thine alabaster cities gleam / Undimmed by human tears!" brings to my mind the indomitable spirit of a great city, and the twin columns of light that appeared as a memorial to those who lost their lives on September 11, 2001. The memorial reminded all of us that our hopes and dreams for the future would not be dimmed!

America! America!

CANYON DE CHELLY NATIONAL MONUMENT, ARIZONA Canyon de Chelly is the home of the Navajo, whose ancestors occupied cliff dwellings in this sacred place. There has been a human presence here for nearly 2,000 years.

God shed His grace on thee

EVERGLADES NATIONAL PARK, FLORIDA ♦ There is only one Everglades in all the world. President Harry Truman dedicated this special place in Florida as a National Park in 1947. The Everglades is the home of many species of beautiful birds, the alligator, and the Florida panther.

From sea to shining sea!

FALMOUTH, MASSACHUSETTS ♦ Katharine Lee Bates was born August 12, 1859, in Falmouth, Massachusetts, on Cape Cod. The Nobska Light stands at Woods Hole (part of Falmouth). Its light shines from sea to shining sea!

Back Cover

YELLOWSTONE NATIONAL PARK, WYOMING & MONTANA Yellowstone is America's first official National Park, dedicated in 1872. The Lower Falls of the Yellowstone River drop more than 300 feet into the Grand Canyon of the Yellowstone.

AMERICA
The Beautiful

SOME OF AMERICA'S BEAUTIFUL PLACES

1 • HECETA HEAD, OREGON

2 • HALF DOME, YOSEMITE NATIONAL PARK, CALIFORNIA

3 • THE LOWER FALLS OF THE YELLOWSTONE,
YELLOWSTONE NATIONAL PARK, WYOMING & MONTANA

4 • GRAND TETON NATIONAL PARK, WYOMING

5 • CANYON DE CHELLY, ARIZONA

6 • MOUNT RUSHMORE NATIONAL MEMORIAL,
SOUTH DAKOTA

7 • SCOTTS BLUFF NATIONAL MONUMENT, NEBRASKA

8 • GARDEN OF THE GODS, PIKES PEAK, COLORADO

9 • STATE OF KANSAS

10 • THE HILL COUNTRY, TEXAS

11 • CASS COUNTY, IOWA

12 • NORTH OF NATCHEZ, MISSISSIPPI

13 • NIAGARA FALLS, NEW YORK

14 • KITTY HAWK, NORTH CAROLINA

15 • KENNEDY SPACE CENTER, CAPE CANAVERAL, FLORIDA

16 • EVERGLADES NATIONAL PARK, FLORIDA

17 • STATE OF VERMONT

18 • PLIMOTH PLANTATION, PLYMOUTH, MASSACHUSETTS

19 • WOODS HOLE, FALMOUTH, MASSACHUSETTS

20 • WASHINGTON, CONNECTICUT

21 • NEW YORK CITY, NEW YORK

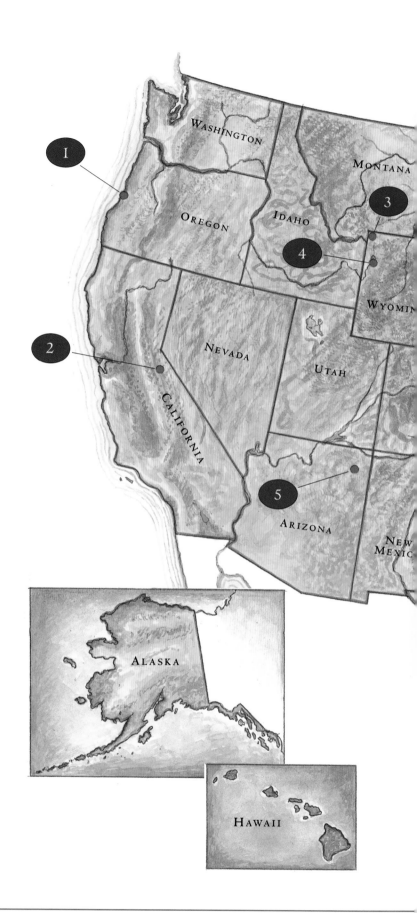

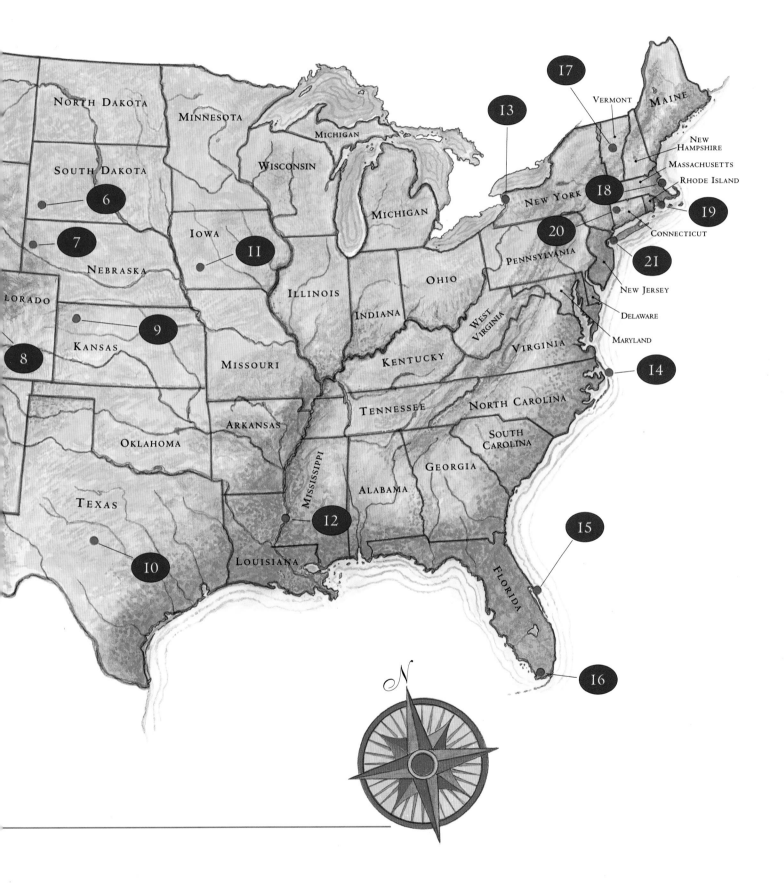

NORTH DAKOTA

MINNESOTA

MICHIGAN

SOUTH DAKOTA

WISCONSIN

6

MICHIGAN

7

IOWA

NEBRASKA

11

LORADO

9

ILLINOIS

OHIO

8

KANSAS

INDIANA

WEST
VIRGINIA

MISSOURI

KENTUCKY

VIRGINIA

TENNESSEE

NORTH CAROLINA

OKLAHOMA

ARKANSAS

SOUTH
CAROLINA

GEORGIA

TEXAS

MISSISSIPPI

ALABAMA

10

LOUISIANA

12

FLORIDA

VERMONT

MAINE

17

13

NEW
HAMPSHIRE

MASSACHUSETTS

NEW YORK

18

RHODE ISLAND

19

PENNSYLVANIA

20

CONNECTICUT

21

NEW JERSEY

DELAWARE

MARYLAND

14

15

16

N

ACKNOWLEDGMENTS

I wish to thank my editor, Nancy Paulsen, for her invitation to create my vision
of this edition of "America the Beautiful." It was an awesome task, indeed, to
create paintings for the poem and song that has been part of our national heritage
since its publication in 1895.

I am grateful for Lynn Sherr's outstanding book, *America the Beautiful:
The Stirring True Story Behind Our Nation's Favorite Song* (PublicAffairs, 2001).
Ms. Sherr's insights as to the meaning of Katharine Lee Bates's words for
"America the Beautiful" gave me a clear direction for my pictorial interpretation.

I would like to thank my friends Robert Shaw and Jason Lindsey, two very
fine nature and wildlife photographers, for allowing me access to their extensive
collections when my personal archives did not suffice. For historical reference,
I am grateful to the following: National Archives, U.S. Geological Survey Collection
(John F. Hillers, *Canyon de Chelly*, 1882), Grant Heilman Photography Inc.
(J. W. MacManigal, *Farmer*, ca. 1930), the Ed Vebell Collection, and NASA
(*Discovery, STS 26*, 1988).

A special thanks to my art director, Cecilia Yung, and designer, Gunta Alexander,
for their exceptional talents and patience on this project. Thanks also to Ed Corvelli
and Phoenix Color Inc. for putting our collective effort into its final printed form.

WENDELL MINOR